THROUGH IT ALL, I'M GOING TO MAKE IT

A Collection of Poetry

Patrice Wilkerson

Patrice Wilkerson
200 White House Road
Nelson, VA 24580

patrice_wilkerson@yahoo.com

October 2018

Printed and bound in the United States of
America

Library of Congress Control Number
2010926890

ISBN: 978-1-729638255

Through It All, I'm Going to Make It
By Patrice D. Wilkerson

2

Dedication

I dedicate my book to God and my wonderful family. I thank God for everything that He has blessed me with. I thank Him for my family, my health and strength, and the talent that He has given me. I know that without Him none of this would be possible. I want to dedicate this book to my father who has passed away. He was such a wonderful man and his untimely passing taught me that tomorrow is not promised. I realized that I need to work harder to fulfill my dreams because you never know when it's your time. I have always wanted to publish a book of poetry but never thought I could do it. I know that with God on my side anything is possible. I also dedicate this book to my family who always supports and encourages me to fulfill my dreams. Mom, I have watched you work hard for so many years. I want you to know, you are my role model. Everything I do is for my family. I love you all!

4

THROUGH IT ALL, I'M GOING TO MAKE IT

Table of Contents

CHAPTER 1:

DEATH COMES KNOCKING

Before I Wake

If I shall die before I wake
I pray the Lord forgives me for all of my
mistakes
I ask that you continue to take care of my
family
And be with me as they mourn the loss of
me
May the words that I have ever written will
touch someone
If they did I know my work here is done
I hope that my smile had brightened
someone's day
And that people found happiness in what I
had to say
I hope that I was able to make a difference
somehow someway
And to all the little girls out there I hope that
I was a role model to many
To my family and friends you were a great
influence to me
Please remember me-keep me in your hearts
I love each and every one of you-my time
has come to depart

If We Were To Never Meet Again

If I were to never see tomorrow
I would thank God for all of life's happiness
and sorrow
I would thank Him for all the blessings
And the knowledge I've gained through
life's lessons

If I were to leave you, mom
Just know, I wish we could have spent more
time together
I wish our days could have lasted forever
You've done so much for our family
You always taught me to hold my head up
high and believe
You worked so hard-what seems a lifetime
Life comes and goes so fast, I wish I could
press rewind
I love you, and just know, all your hard
work will pay off in due time
I know we didn't get to say goodbye
Just whenever you think of me, look for me
in the sky

If I were to leave you, dad
Just know, I won't forget all the good times
we had
How I always wanted to make you laugh
You're very protective of your little girl

So afraid to let her go in this cold gruesome
world
I know it's hard, but try to keep it together
Cherish our memories-for they will last
forever
I know we didn't get to say goodbye
Just whenever you think of me, look for me
in the sky

If He came for me right this moment
Just know, I'll protect you everywhere you
go
I thank you for the precious times
Day and night, night and day you were
always on my mind
I thank you for showing me how to be a
good friend
If we were to never meet again
Promise me that your love for me will never
end
I thank you for believing in me
I thank you for the love and support you
have given me
I know we didn't get to say goodbye
Just whenever you think of me, look for me
in the sky

To everyone:
Cherish the people around you-tomorrow is
not promised

To My Beloved Papa

Dear Papa, my grandfather, my inspiration
This is my letter to you, showing my
appreciation
I will remember all the laughs, hugs, and
even your kiss
Without any doubt you will be missed
It's going to be hard with you not around
But it's good to know you're in heaven
watching down
I want you to know you were a great
granddad
You were there for me through the good
times and bad
Words cannot express how much I will miss
you
It's going to be tough but we will pull
through
You will be remembered and NEVER
forgotten
Making sure your grandchildren were
spoiled rotten
We will never be apart; this is straight from
my heart
You're in heaven now carrying out your part

Come Back to Me

Since you have been gone things haven't
been the same
I would give anything to hear you call my
name
For the sake of the family, I'm staying
strong
It's hard for me to grasp the fact that you are
gone
Papa, my eyes filled with tears the day that
you passed
Your disease took a toll on your mind
extremely fast
The whole family misses you
We're having a hard time but I know we'll
make it through
Papa, you meant so much to me and much
more
I would love to see you one day walk
through our front door
You are no longer suffering; I know you are
being taken care of
I can see your smiling face looking down
from above
Memories of me sitting on your lap having
good times
You were a wonderful person-always
sincere and kind
Without you, my life feels so empty
Papa, would you please come back to me

For Granted

With the snap of a finger, my life flashed
before my eyes
How could this be; I didn't say my last
goodbyes
A few moments ago, everything was just
fine
Five minutes later, a car crashed into mine
Pain, anxiety, and fear-is what I was feeling
I'm alive by God's grace-is what I was
thinking
Dear Lord, I came close but you kept me
here
You kept me safe and secure-despite my
fear
Thanking you for dear life, to you I pray
Your grace kept me here another day
As I saw the car crash into me
I thought; there's so much more I want to do
and see
We sometimes think we're going to live
forever-and that's not the case
Live each day to the fullest, don't let a
moment waste
If you got a dream, work hard to make it
come true
Just pray and believe-the rest is all up to you

A Tragic Life

It's been a while since I last saw you
Your face filled with joy-is how I last
remember you
You had dreams of some day becoming
somebody
Leaving this small town life, in which you
thought you were just a nobody
In my eyes you were truly special-I just wish
you could see
You had the talent and the drive to be
anything you wished to be
But instead you chose to drink your life
away
In the midst of that I saw your hopes and
dreams wash away
I wish you had of been stronger-but fell into
the trap of the nightlife and party scene
It didn't take you long to realize the highlife
isn't so cool as it may seem
I wish your family had of guided you in a
better light
Frustrated-you were dying to leave the
house, just waiting to be sure the time was
right
This tragic night I wish you hadn't got into
this mess
It was obvious to me that you drank because
you were depressed

Drunk out of your mind you decided to get
behind the wheel
Tragically in moments you were killed
As soon as I heard the news I couldn't
believe what I was hearing
My eyes quickly began tearing
You were so young and had everything to
live for
I wish you could have heard all the
opportunities that were knocking at your
door
Now we'll never know what you could have
been
Until then, I want you to know I miss my
friend

Motherless Child

There once was a young pretty girl
Who had dreams of traveling across the
world
She longed for attention from her mother
So she searched for love from others
This would soon become addictive
To strangers she had a lot of love to give
She ran around with men who could care
less
Unhappy with her life and how it became
this terrible mess
She wanted to gain back control of her life
Maybe settle down become a mother and
wife
She suddenly changed her ways
And she promised never go back to her self-
destructing phase
She was in a better place, things were finally
looking up
Until one day she decided to go for a check
up
The doctor delivers bad news that sends
chills down her spine
You have HIV-puzzled she replies, what do
you mean, I feel just fine?
She went home that day feeling worthless
She later gave her life to Christ and learned
to make the best

From that moment on she felt hopeful not hopeless
Sadly, on October 7, 2005 this pretty young girl was laid to rest

A Beautiful Pair

My eyes filled with joy the day you two
were born
Minutes later my eyes are filled with tears as
I mourn
Your loss is something I have yet to deal
with
How can God take away such a precious
gift?
I lost myself when you passed away
I have no passion for life no words to say
I lost my first niece and nephew - oh how I
miss you
I would give anything and everything for the
chance to see you
It's hard to get my heart back in one piece
I will love you forever and always, my
beautiful nephew and niece

Dear Daddy

How could I forget the morning of May 28,
2008-it was quite a scare
I watched you pass out in the living room
floor-you were lying helplessly there
Thoughts ran through my mind, is this it
Is this all the time that we get
I didn't get to say goodbye to you
I didn't get to tell you how much I love and
care for you
Quickly I got on my knees and asked God to
bring you back to me
I just couldn't imagine my life without my
dearest daddy
You were there for me through it all
Dear Lord please, answer my call
As the ambulance came and checked you
out
The Lord answered my call-without a
shadow of doubt
You brought him back to me
Dear daddy, as you lay awake I want you to
know
I love how our relationship continues to
grow
It sometimes has been rocky
But I know now that you just wanted the
best for me
I appreciate all the kind things you have
done for me

I'm here to take care of you-whatever you
need I'll do
My dearest daddy, I know I don't say this
much but-I love you

Dearest Daddy

You are truly the best father anyone can
have
We are going to miss your hugs, kisses, and
your laugh
Our minds keep telling us you are in a better
place
But our hearts long to see your beautiful
face
You are genuinely one of a kind
You are the sweetest, funniest, and most
caring person anyone could ever find
Everyone knows we all share something
very special
We have this bond that is truly unbreakable
You were so proud of all of our
achievements
You were always there for the good and the
bad moments
Don't worry, we'll tell D.J. how wonderful a
man you were
We will all cherish your memories forever
God wanted you; He saw fit to set you free
We miss you and we love you, our dearest
daddy

The Greatest Pain

It was a week ago today I buried my father,
my hero, my best friend
The one who I thought would stick around
until the very end
I always pictured you would be the one
crying at my funeral
The fact that you are no longer here is so
unbelievable
Every waking moment-I long to see you
walk through that door
Every day that you are gone-makes me love
you that much more
My days are filled with emptiness,
confusion, and anger
Your handsome face is all that my mind
seems to remember
In all my life I've never felt this much pain
There are no sunny days-just rain
People try to cheer me up, but it's not much
they can say or do
They have no clue all that we went through
We had a bond that no one could possibly
understand
I would give anything to simply touch your
hand
Every day is just-another day
And everyone always asks, are you okay
Truthfully I'm not-I'm dying in the outside
and in

And I won't feel complete-until I see my father again.

Gone, not Forgotten

Daddy, it's been weeks since you have
passed
All my mind remembers is me seeing you
last
I miss seeing you in your favorite chair
The fact that you are gone is so unfair
Although you are not here-we will not forget
you
We will lift up your name in everything that
we do
Your spirit will forever live on through me
and the rest of the family
But that doesn't compare-cause it's your
face I would rather see
I visit your grave every chance I can
You were truly a wonderful and
hardworking man
I won't forget all the precious times we
shared
We sometimes bickered-but that showed me
how much you cared
I would give anything to have you back in
my life
I'm trying to stay strong for the rest of your
children and wife
I miss making you laugh and all the good
times
Each and every day my mind seems to press
rewind

To your last days, I wish there was more that
could have been said
I just can't come to terms with the fact that
you are dead
You and I share something so special-we
have this special bond
Daddy, you are gone but not forgotten-your
spirit will forever live on.

Still Your Girl

I know we are no longer together, but in my
mind; I'm still your girl
You are the only man for me in this whole
wide world
Why did you have to leave, what did I do
wrong?
Being here with me is where you belong
I never got to tell you how much I loved you
unconditionally
I would do anything just to see you happy
Sure we had our ups and downs, but now I
realize
You were simply trying to protect me from
those creepy guys
Everybody knew we were like Bonnie and
Clyde
And if you would come back to me today,
I'll gladly stretch my arms out wide
You see he left me on June 18, 2008
Out of all the 365 days – this is the one I
truly hate
You were sick but no one expected you to
die
And ever since that day I've been asking
myself why
For the past year and a half my life has felt
incomplete
I know it's going to be a joyous occasion
when we finally meet

For 25 years you were my best friend, my
rock, you meant everything to me
Even though you are no longer around I will
always be your girl, I love you daddy

My Heavenly Angels

I have so many angels watching me from
above
They include my daddy, papa, uncle, aunt,
and friend, who I miss and love
I am never alone because I know they are
always around me
Although their faces, well I wish I could see
However, I can feel their spirit surrounding
me constantly
Just the other night, I could feel my dad
sitting on my bed
I can remember when he put my bed
together, his second home was his tool shed
I could also feel my friend Johnsie around
me in Sunday school as I read
She was a Sunday school teacher, "Sunday
School sets the groundwork for God's
teachings," that's what she always said
Just the other Saturday, my Papa rode with
me as I drove to Emporia safely
Jack of all trade, we all knew him as John
Dee
My aunt Susie goes with me to work to
make sure I press the right key
She excelled in school, making straight A's
yearly
My uncle Wayne sits right beside me when I
watch the basketball games on TV

He was the sports fanatic out of the whole
family
As you can see they follow me around all of
the time
They give me love, guidance, and peace of
mind
I love my heavenly angels; they are the best
you will ever find

CHAPTER 2:

LIFE'S TRIALS
AND
TRIBULATIONS

One of my Bad Days

Today is July 22, 2008-one of my bad days
How do I feel-well I miss my dad in so
many ways
Some days are better than others but this day
especially- I feel beside myself
I miss my hero, companion, this I cannot
help
It hurts coming home and you are nowhere
to be found
We sure miss having you around
It's hard to get over something so
devastating such as this
Your smile, your sense of humor-everything
about you we sure are going to miss
What am I going to do without you by my
side
It's like my heart stopped beating the day
that you died
All day people kept asking what's wrong,
what's wrong
I simply say-I'm just tired I don't want to
make my story long
I sadly stare at your favorite chair
How badly I wish you were sitting there
They say things get better with time-I don't
see how could
Some days are better than others-but today
I'm just not doing so good.

Poet's Pain

I can't stop them falling no matter how hard
I try
My emotions and feelings-deep down inside
makes me wanna cry
Lord, why am I so sad, you have blessed me
abundantly?
But my days are filled with gloom-my
nights are cold and empty
I got some deep issues I try hard to conceal
I got a lot of pain in my heart, only you and
I can feel
Well for starters, I lost a man who truly
means the world to me
I need him here now, like I need air to
breathe
I could never imagine losing someone so
dear
I never been afraid of death, however
loneliness I do fear
Everyone always said how much I look like
you and act like you
I would give anything and everything just to
simply talk to you
I wish things could go back to the way they
were before
I miss from seeing you watch over us at
night from our bedroom door
I have my good days and bad days

But hopefully this poet's pain would not last always

This brings me to my next issue... I have a
friend who makes me truly happy
However we live miles apart and those eyes
I barely see
It's so hard when you want that person so
bad to be there
That's when I come to realize that life
sometimes don't seem fair
Sometimes my sadness comes from us not
being together
What keeps me going are the memories-how
I love to remember
I have my good days and bad days
But hopefully this poet's pain would not last
always

Have you ever felt like you are not living up
to your potential?
Success, love, and happiness, are very key
essentials
I got champagne dreams with barely beer
money
I live paycheck to paycheck and have to
borrow from my mom's, now ain't that
funny
I bust my butt everyday and somehow it
doesn't all make sense

But I know my time is coming the Lord has
a funny way of dropping hints
2009, I'm making it my year
I plan to transform my tears into love,
happiness, and a brand new career
I have my good days and bad days
But hopefully this poet's pain would not last
always

Tearful Eyes

Every day I think about you
Wondering when is the next time I can see
my beautiful boo
I'm ecstatic when we are together
Wishing that special moment could last
forever
Happiness and joy is what I always feel
My broken heart-something only you can
heal
How do you live without your true love by
your side?
Sadness and loneliness-something I can no
longer hide
You are my sun, my moon, and even my
shining star
I wish my love wasn't so far
At night, I pretend you are lying with me
I miss your touch, your smile, and especially
your beauty
I long for the day we shall meet again
I'll always love you forever and ever-The
End

You're Sorry

I've heard these words so many times before
You say you're sorry, but then you hurt me
ten times more
I'm tired and in pain, saying sorry just can't
make it right
You tell me you love me, but we end up
fighting the same fight
I want to forgive you, but how do I know
you mean what you say
I know the past is the past and today is a
new day
But I love you and I would never try to hurt
you, obviously you don't feel the same way
Should I stay and wait for you to change or
say my final goodbyes
Do you mean what you say, or is this
another one of your many lies?
I used to wonder why do you treat me this
way- was it me?
Indeed it was, all this time I blamed you
when I should have blamed myself- you see
It was me that allowed you to treat me
badly, lie continually, and cry constantly
I admit, I did it to myself, not you
Because I allowed all the pain you caused to
continue
But no more, the buck stops here
It's a brand new me, a brand new attitude,
and oh yeah, a brand new year

I'm done and this time it's for real
Because when you love someone, being hurt
is not part of the deal
You never really listened to what I had to
say
So I'll make it short and sweet, goodbye,
and that's all I have to say

Nickname is Crazy

I've been called crazy so many times
People think I'm 'bout to lose my mind
I think I'm normal-they just don't
understand me
Why can't I be accepted for the person I
choose to be
I personally, don't think there's anything
wrong
I realize I'm not like the others, which
makes me feel like I don't belong
But I'm not weird-I just think and act in a
different way
Sometimes people laugh at the silly things I
say
It's like no one ever takes me seriously
A lot of times they just end up calling me
crazy
I admit I'm very unique-but that's okay
Everyone is entitled to be themselves-aren't
they?
I'm one in a million and boy am I proud
I'm soft spoken and kind, not obnoxious and
loud
I have the heart of gold
And the patience of Job-so I have been told
I'm the sweetest person you would ever
want to meet
I don't look crazy either-I make sure my
clothes are nice and neat

I'm a good person-just give me a chance
I have no rhythm, but I love to dance
I'm not as crazy as everyone thinks I may be
I challenge you to someday sit down and get
to know the real me

She

She was brought up in the church and raised
the right way
She talked proper and always knew the right
words to say
She always put on a smile even though she
was dying inside
As if all her hopes and aspirations suddenly
died
She couldn't understand the cause of her
unhappiness
She felt as though her life was filled with
nothing but emptiness
She was searching for something but didn't
quite know what it was
Deep down inside she was unsure of who
she was
Longing for love and affection
Her search would definitely lead her in the
wrong direction
She gained confidence for all the wrong
reasons
Men came and went similar to the seasons
She thought she found happiness but then
her emptiness grew
Her friends and family felt they lost her-this
wasn't the same girl they knew
She was lost but then found herself
She learned before you let anyone love you-
you have to love yourself

Soon after that she found love for all the
right reasons
And this person has stuck with her for the
past 20 seasons
She's happy now and her soul lives again
She feels like God gave her a second chance
and she has learned to cherish life until the
end

Keep Your Innocence

I wish I saw more little girls
The ones who still plays with dolls and wear
curls
I wish young girls were not so eager to
become women
So fast to run around with much older men
If you know like I know you will want to
stay a child
Instead of being fast and running wild
Young girls-please realize this world is not
for you
What if you get pregnant-then what will you
do?
A baby raising a baby-how cute is that
It makes you wonder, where were the
parents at
Young girls don't rush your life away
These adult games are not for you to play
Just focus on being a child and having a
good time
Your childhood is not something you can
just press rewind
Young girls-don't let a man determine your
fate
Keep your innocence baby girl, it's well
worth the wait

Behind the Smiles

If one would look at you, it seems like you
have it all together
Reality is, things could be better
Behind your smiles lies unhappiness
Your heart and soul is filled with emptiness
All your hopes and dreams seem to have
faded away
When you wake, you hope that today will be
a better day
Life feels hopeless, you have nowhere to
turn
Give your life to Christ and see what you
will learn
He gives you joy in the morning, night, and
noonday
When life gets rough, fall on your knees and
pray
He may not come right then but He'll be
there right on time
He is the greatest companion you will ever
find
He makes you feel fortunate to be alive
Once you let Him into your life, He is sure
to make things better
Once you give your life to Him, He
promises to stay with you forever
Give him a chance and He'll show you what
real love is about

And next time you smile-you're smiling on
the inside and out

Artificial

In this busy world we all need a little bit of
quietness;
Sometimes in certain situations its best
But in my world sometimes it's all I know
It used to not be like this, especially a couple
years ago
I was always surrounded, no matter which
way I would turn
It was never quiet, I never got a chance to
think, grow, or learn
Artificial- was who I was surrounded by
People who didn't care if I were to live or
die
But still I knew, I just didn't care
I was trying to hide the grief that I bear
I eventually said goodbye to the friends I
had
The more I sit and the more I think, being
alone isn't so bad
I mean, after all I have God, my family, and
my close friend
Whom I know I can depend
I've had to say a lot of goodbyes
But in the end I realized, it's not about how
much you socialize
It's all about surrounding yourself with
positivity
And getting rid of the negativity

But it's up to you to determine the good and
bad seed
Because when you succeed, wouldn't you
want to have people around you that always
believed?

Many Faces

Long ago, my best friend had more than one
face
Looking back, how could I have been so
naïve for 4 years, what a waste
Funny, cool, and likeable was the face I
grew to know
Second face-I learned was not my friend but
my foe
You can imagine my hurt upon finding out
Being stabbed in the back by my best friend-
what was this all about?
I had to get to the bottom of things
In denial I was, maybe things aren't what
they seem
I couldn't let her go-how dumb was I
You were no good for me-why couldn't I
tell you bye?
Yeah, we had been through a lot of stuff
together
But I couldn't take being around someone
fake forever
What did I do wrong-is what I would sit and
ponder
Absolutely nothing, I realized there are
millions of people just like her
You gotta learn how to tell the real from the
fake
It's not about how many friends you can
make

In the beginning, you might not notice how
many faces they may have
The first face-is always the kind that makes
you feel good and laugh
But the second is the one you need to watch
closely
It's about recognizing that some people
aren't who they claim to be
If you are ever in this situation-just know
it's not healthy
Always remember to do what's best for you
only

To Everyone:
Don't hold on to someone who is going to
bring you down

CHAPTER 3:

MY FAMILY, MY STRENGTH

Lady of the House

Dear Mom, you have always been a strong
woman-that's for sure
Anytime we would ever have a problem-you
had the magic cure
You are a tremendous leader, independent,
and very smart
You've held the family down right from the
start
I know it's been rough since dad passed
It seems like everything happened so fast
You not only lost your husband but your
best friend
And like a good woman you stuck by him
until the very end
But you remain strong just like always
And just like the rest of us you have your
good days and bad days
I admire you, throughout the pain and the
hurt, your strength still shines through
And you know what, when I grow up I
definitely want to be just like you
You taught me that in life it's not always
what you wanna do, but what you have to do
For so many years I watched you work your
life away
And I would pray and pray for a brighter
day
I'm saddened that things had to turn out this
way

But if I could hear dad's voice I bet I know
just what he would say
Princess, you are doing a good job keeping
the family together, stay strong and I look
forward to seeing you some day
Love you forever and always

Like Mother, Like Daughter

Mother-you worked so hard to provide for
your family
You have sacrificed so much just so we can
be happy
You've missed a lot of good times through
the years
Every time we have to say goodbye my eyes
fill with tears
I long for the day we could spend more time
together
Watching television with you and lying
beside you are pastimes I love to remember
I wish I can hold on tight to you and be with
you forever
Your strength, leadership, and knowledge
admires me
Just like you, everything I do is for my
family
When I make it big I'll see to it that all your
dreams are fulfilled
I'll see to it that you will never have to pay
another bill
I want to give you everything you have
given me
I want to take you places you never dreamed
you'll see
Just like you, I know you got to work hard if
you want nice things

Just like you, I won't stop until I fulfill my
dreams
Just like you, I know that you won't get far
by sitting on your behind
Just like you, I know that life can be
challenging and unkind
Like mother, like daughter as they
sometimes say
Mother-you are truly admirable in every
way

A Beautiful Gift

I received my gift on March 8, 2008
Derek Antonio Wilkerson, Jr. - you were
well worth the wait
This little bundle of joy have finally entered
into my life
How excited I was for my family, my
brother, and his wife
You have definitely changed my life for the
better
There were plenty tearful nights-oh how I
can remember
When I'm with you nothing else even
matters to me
It's your smile and beautiful brown eyes I
long to see
When I make you smile-something comes
over me
It's nice to have someone to love me
unconditionally
I come to tears whenever I have to leave you
Wondering when's the next time I can see
you-especially in your favorite color blue
Plenty nights we prayed for your safe arrival
The whole concept of me being an auntie-
how unbelievable
I thank God each and everyday
For my beautiful gift, Mr. Derek Antonio
Wilkerson, Jr. - or as we call him D.J.

Dear Sister

It feels like just yesterday I held you into my
arms-you were the most beautiful baby
Now, I can't believe you are almost a young
lady
My, how the time has passed
It's like you grew up so fast
I want to protect you and keep you away
from bad things
I want to show you all the joy that life may
bring
Everything I do is for you, please keep in
mind
I'll hold you down until the end of time
I've always told you-you are so special, one
of a kind
Your personality and charisma is a favorite
of mine
I see a lot of potential in you, which I hope
you see
I admire how you steer away from
negativity
I may push you sometimes but I just want
the best for you
I may not tell you a lot but just know I love
you

My Brother, My Big Brother

It seemed like just yesterday we were
playing outside on the swing set
But let's rewind a little further to the first
day we met
It was June 23, 1983-I was barely a day old
You tried to hit me in the head with your
bottle-so I was told
I could tell you really didn't like me-but I
couldn't really blame you
For all this time you were the baby-all the
attention was centered on you
But throughout the years we grew to be so
close
Thinking back it was your protectiveness
that I loved the most
I enjoyed riding to school with you when
you got your first car
Whenever I would wonder off you would
say "come back you are going too far"
You have been a great role model for Chris
and I
You are a great husband and father; overall
you're such a remarkable guy
Even in darkness your spirituality still shines
through
The world will be a much better place if
more men were made like you
Big brother, I thank you for always chasing
my fears away

If anyone every ask me just who you are, I'll
proudly say
That's my brother, my big brother, all day
every day

Familiar Stranger

I have known about you for quite some time
now
The fact of having another family member-I
can't grasp how
I'm sure you are quite a character just like
the rest of the family
For years I've wondered about your
existence –who really is she
But finally knowing the truth has definitely
set me free
I'm not quite sure I really want to meet you
Let's be honest I barely even know you
I contemplate would he want us to meet-or
keep things the way they were
My mind says no but my heart says-yes I
would like to get to know her
Will I cherish every moment
Or will you just bring sadness and
disappointment
I wonder do you even resemble us
Between him and her was it love or just lust
When, where, how-could all this happen
I find it hard to believe that that we could
actually be kin
Should I or shouldn't I build a relationship
Don't keep things in the dark because pretty
soon it shall come to light-just a tip.

Family Ain't Family

Whatever happened to the good old days
When you got together at Grandma's house
on Sundays
Where everyone would laugh and talk, we'll
have so much fun
And the grownups couldn't eat until all the
kids were done
My uncle would take all of us kids to the
store right after supper
And we'll come back to Grandma's and
have a good time playing with each other
But these good times seemed to have just
faded away
And it's only a handful at Grandma's on
Sundays
I barely see my cousins we all used to be so
close
Especially my cousin who I enjoyed the
most
Now our Sundays are reduced to special
occasions only
We need to be mindful that in life family is
key
We can't take Grandma's house for granted
as if she'll be there always
Let's love one another as if we were in our
last days
Family aren't as close as they used to be
Family just ain't family

My First Christmas

It's Christmas, the gifts have been brought
and everyone is filled with cheer
However, as I awake, my eyes are filled
with sadness and tears
This Christmas will definitely be different
from last year
It will be my first Christmas without my
daddy being here
I had made plans to go to Granny's house
with the rest of the family
But I couldn't push myself to go, simply
because you wouldn't be there with me
I know you are watching from above, but I
need you here with me
All I want for Christmas is you daddy
But I know that's impossible-God needs you
up there instead
As each day comes and goes your precious
face runs through my head
"I'm not going to always be here," that you
said
Who would have thought that last Christmas
was our last Christmas?
Dearest daddy, I love you, Merry Christmas

It's Christmas day and I'm on my way to see
my pride and joy
His name is D.J., my baby nephew; I'm
excited to see him open up his toys

You see this is his very first Christmas-and
we want it to be a special one
My excitement lies in seeing him having fun
I hope you enjoy your very first Christmas
Dearest D.J., I love you, Merry Christmas

To Daddy and D.J.:
This Christmas will be my first Christmas
without you
But also, this Christmas will be my first
Christmas with my baby nephew
I love you both in very special ways
To all Merry Christmas and Happy Holidays

Money Changes

Everything was all good just a year ago
As the family gathered for your retirement,
you were so happy-how do I know
Well, for starters you had a smile as big as
the rainbow
You stood tall and proud-we all considered
you our hero
As time changed, we noticed a difference
Family functions, sad to say but we rarely
see you
The stories that I'm hearing I hope aren't
true
Your life is fixated on giving your wife and
child the world
But truthfully speaking they need to grow up
and be a big boy and girl
When I see you your face is filled with
worry and hopelessness
I truly miss the old you-remember without
all the money and stress
They say money makes the world go round
Well, I've seen money bring people up and
also bring people down
Don't lose yourself keep God first, then
family, and friends who are true
I can honestly say money has not changed
me, what about you?

Sunday

The most complicated day for me would
have to be Sunday
This is when I attend church and afterwards,
go to my grandma's house to relax and play
When dinner is ready, we all gather around
the table and pray
It's a joyous occasion for all-the soul food,
the conversations, and most importantly the
family
Overall, grandma's house is the best place to
be
But as the sun goes down we know that the
good times are about to end
We can't wait for next Sunday to do it all
over again
While Sundays bring joy-it also brings a bit
of sadness to me
I have a best friend who I occasionally get to
see
We have the best time-I enjoy every minute
that we spend together
I wish this perfect moment could last forever
But when Sunday comes, we know the fun
is about to end
Because God only knows when we will see
each other again
It's hard being away from someone who is
such a good friend

As we say goodbye the tears start rolling
down my cheeks
Because I know that I won't feel this
complete again, until another two more
weeks
When I get home the memories start to play
back in my mind
If only I could press rewind
I'll see to it that we are together for a
lifetime
But until then I'll keep praying that our
Sundays are filled with nothing but laughter
instead of choked up goodbyes
I dread Sundays because the thought of
leaving you makes me wanna cry
However, I look forward to Sundays
because I get to smell grandma's homemade
apple pie
Even though Sundays are full of some lows
and many highs
It's a day that is dedicated to that powerful
man in the sky

Reunion

This special occasion only comes once a
year
People are filled with laughter and good
cheer
We are so glad to see each other
Not wanting to ever leave one another
The kids are playing
While the grown folk are reminiscing
There's plenty of food for everyone
The air is filled with laughter and fun
You wish that day could last forever
Because you don't know the next time you
all will be together
As we all say our heartfelt goodbyes, we
each shed a tear
I love my family always and forever-until
next year

CHAPTER 4:

LOVE AND HAPPINESS

A Love in the Sky

I'm in love with a man, whom I can't even
see
But I know He loves me unconditionally
He listens, encourages, and empowers me
Although there are times when we might
disagree
However, I never question His decisions
because I know He only wants the best for
me
I never feel alone because He's always there
He's with me as I sleep at night and even
when I wake up to comb my hair
He always forgives me despite my many
sins
I place Him above my family and my friends
He is there with me throughout the good
times and bad
He even consoled me when I had lost my
dad
And oh yeah, He's jealous and
overprotective, which is what I love most of
all
He's always around me – He even catches
me when I fall
To my love in the sky – you're all I need in
this world
You're my man and I'm your girl

Our Love Story

I can't forget the day that we met each other
It was fate how we bumped into each other
I never thought how close we would become
It's like you knew exactly where I was
coming from
I knew you were the one for me
Sharing this with my friends didn't come so
easily
What do you mean you love him, you guys
used to hate each other?
My reply, sometimes the good ones are last
to discover
Jealousy, was all that was around us
Hard to escape the negativity that
surrounded us
You and I were falling apart at the seams
All we did was argue and scream
We had to separate ourselves from the
negativity
I couldn't believe my friends didn't want the
best for me
We knew we loved each other more than
anything else
Our feelings towards each other were
definitely heartfelt
We ended up saying goodbye
To the crew, because once you grow up you
realize

The difference between true friends and true
lies
Our love has been stronger ever since then
This is our love story, the end

On this Day

I can't believe how long it's been
2 years and 13 days, as my lover and friend
We guided each other through the rocky
times
Not one memory that we've shared seems to
slip my mind
Ever so striking-your intelligence and
beauty
A match made in heaven-wouldn't you
agree?
I lose myself when looking into your eyes
Especially when they cry-as we say our
goodbyes
You mean the world to me
You are my one and my only
On this day, will you marry me?

Happy Anniversary

Well, another year has passed
It took a lot of hard work but we made our
relationship last
We had a lot of obstacles but we stuck it out
We taught each other what real love is about
I look forward to spending my life with you
I could tell you a million times how much I
love you
You are exactly what I wished for
On this day, I wish you a Happy
Anniversary and many more

My Addiction

From the moment I glanced at you-
I knew I was hooked
All these years love was staring right in
front of me-
If only I had of looked
You waited patiently and when I finally
gave in
My life changed for the better and I was
forgiven for my sins
From that moment on I knew I couldn't live
without you
Day and night, night and day all I think
about is being with you
When there is darkness-you are my light
When life feels like a battle-you are there to
help me fight
You are my medicine-when I feel pain
You are my sunshine-when there is rain
You keep me safe in stormy weather
I'm at my happiest when we are together
Your smile, intelligence, and beauty-is what
I love about you
Question is how can I live without you?
The truth is I can't-I'm addicted to you in so
many ways
You are my life, my soul, my everything-I
Love You Always

Valentine

I have liked you for a while, this you may
not know
My feelings for you I'm too scared to show
When I see you my heart beats faster and
faster
I daydream about me and you being happily
ever after
The way I feel about you is true
My promise, I won't do anything to hurt you
I'll be your shoulder if you need one to cry
on
If you ever weak, for you I'll be strong
Every night I pray that one day you'll be
mine
Won't you please be my valentine?

Strange Love

You stole my heart right from the beginning
I couldn't imagine all the joy you would
bring
Everything felt so right for that moment
It felt like you were heaven sent
You had your flaws but I thought I could
look past
I worked so hard to try to make our love last
You wanted to control me and yet I allowed
you
I loved you but at the same time I hated you
And also I hated me; I never knew I could
be so weak
But you'll do anything if its love that you
are trying to seek
I tried to get out but I was afraid of you
You would get so angry-I was scared of
what you might do
And then someone else came in the picture
and showed me the light
Love should feel good, not be an everyday
fight
Jealous you were but you lost out
Controlling someone is not what love is
about
I'll pray for you, but also I thank you
I regret the fact that I ever loved you

As Much As I Love You

We've been together for what seems a
lifetime
You love how I finish your sentences and
you finish mine
We complement each other very well
Truly we love each other, that's not hard to
tell
But there are some questions I would like
answers to
Do you love me as much as I love you
Do you constantly dream of the day we say I
do
Do you pray for me as much as I pray for
you
Do anyone else's love surpass the love I
have for you
Do you tell me you love me as much as I tell
you
Are you down for me as much as I'm down
for you
Would you die for me as I would you
Do you cherish me the same as I cherish you
Do you understand me as much as I
understand you
I love you more than life itself
But sometimes I feel like I'm in a
relationship all by myself
Sometimes we may take people for granted-
as if their life will never end

Love me now as much as I love you-don't
wait till the very end

Blessed To Have You

You brighten my day with your beautiful
smile
Glazing into your eyes makes every moment
worthwhile
I think about you every hour, every moment
of each day
You have impacted my life in so many ways
When I go a while without seeing you-I tend
to lose my mind
I'm blessed to have you because you are
loving, caring, and kind
You asked me to be your girl-I believe it
was the 6th day of December
I have enjoyed each and every moment that
we have spent together
You are a great friend and a wonderful lover
I am committed to you always and forever
We both have grown spiritually and
mentally
It's obvious that you are the best person for
me
Words cannot express the way I feel
I am blessed to finally find a love that is real
Things have not always been great but we
made it through
I love you and I'm thankful and blessed to
have you

Life

Living in today's world there are all kinds of
people you may meet
Well this is a story about a woman named
Sarah, who frequently gets beat
She came from a broken home and never
really knew what real love was
For some reason she attracts men who abuse
her just because
Sarah thinks she's in love-I don't see how
The man she's in love with calls her names
like-you fat cow
She thinks love is supposed to feel this way
But little does she know love is not getting
abused everyday
Her friends try to talk some sense into her
Sadly Sarah never listened; her body was
laid to rest the 3rd day of September

We need to come together and watch out for
one another
Drugs can take over anyone-your father,
sister, or brother
This is a story about Dave who always felt
empty inside
Seven months ago his devoted mother sadly
had died
He was searching for something that would
ease his pain

Quickly so called friends turned him on to
cocaine
He soon fell in love with the "high"
His real friends tried to tell him from this
you could possibly die
He didn't care he thought he found what he
was searching for
He continued to use cocaine more and more
Sadly he didn't make it past his 23rd birthday
He was laid to rest the 7th day of May

Sometimes people may not get love and
attention from home-so they search
elsewhere for it
A lot of times it's the wrong love and
attention that they may get
This is the story of Amber who got so
addicted to the wrong attention she started
selling herself
Even though it was the wrong attention, this
is the most she's ever felt
Between time her body is worn out and
she's dying of AIDS; physically and
emotionally this is the greatest pain she's
ever felt
She lived with AIDS two years before it
killed her
This precious soul died the 18th of October
Amber, Dave, and Sarah's story is
something we all may go through

We lose ourselves in searching for
something and don't quite know what it may
lead to
People are searching for love but what they
find is something totally different
In the end all it brings is sadness and
disappointment
A lot of people walk around hurt but act like
everything is just fine
Love yourself first and then real love will
come in due time.

God Bless the Children

When I see little children it's something
about them that brings me great joy
God has a special way of watching over
little girls and little boys
I like to see smiles on their faces
But I know that smiles can turn to frowns in
some cases
I have a friend who had a rough childhood
She had thoughts of killing her mom-if only
she could
Her mom would beat her and call her all
sorts of names
The poor child thought things would get
better-but they remained the same
And somehow she always thought she was
the blame, but it's her mother
Who can't appreciate the beautiful gift God
gave her
She prays and asks God, why, why can't my
mother love me
Will I find out the answer eventually?
I just don't know how much more of this I
can take
Please, make my mom love me, for my sake
It's so many children who go through this
very same thing
Because you have selfish parents who don't
know how much joy a child can bring

A mother's love is something kids shouldn't
have to search for
As each day comes and goes you should
love that child even more
God blessed you with something so special
others would kill for
Take them in your arms, show them how
much you love them
That's the most precious gift you could ever
receive to you, from him

Spring

My favorite season is spring
When the air is fresh and clean
My mother opens the window
While I lay quietly on my pillow
And listen to the birds sing
Beautiful songs of spring

A Fulfilled Life

When I grow up I want to live in a mansion
with ceilings that touch the sky
Fancy restaurants, out of town trips, my oh
my
I'll buy what I want when I want, I just
wouldn't care
My life is going to be so fair

When I grow up I want to find love, possibly
become a wife
I'll make a vow to love you for life
Everyday will be filled with happiness and
laughter
And we will live happily ever after
I'll support your dreams and you'll support
mines
My life is going to be just fine

When I grow up I want to have a big family,
with kids running every which a way
Getting them ready for school and kissing
them good-bye each day
Watching them grow up and listening to
every word they say
My beautiful babies, I'll love them endlessly
Look just how awesome my life is going to
be

I'm going to make sure everything I say
comes true, you'll see
A mansion without a family – think of how
empty that will be
Eating dinner alone – to me sounds pretty
depressing
And if you tell me you love me I better see a
diamond ring
First comes love, then comes marriage, and
well you know the rest
Call me old fashioned but to me this formula
work best
Success plus love equals true happiness.

Who I Am

I'm way too skinny, some folks may say
They think I act and talk in such a white way
I've also been told my eyes are just too big –
I look like a deer caught in headlights
And I have legs like a chicken – I could
never wear tights
My veins bulge out of my arms; some say
it's so disgusting
I'm only 4'11 and 95 pounds – I think I'm
done growing
Just like my granny, I have a little gap in my
smile
I'm 26 years old and people still think I
resemble a child

Sometimes I wish I looked like the girls on
TV
But then I take a look at the mirror and see
my own beauty
I may not be tall enough to be a model, but
I'm happy with the way God made me
I may have big eyes, but I'm blessed God
gave me the gift to see
I may be small in stature, but my hearts is as
big as the blue sea
Even though I may look different, I know
that I am pretty
From my big eyes all the way down to my
big feet

I love who I am…this is me, this is what makes me unique

CHAPTER 5:

WITH GOD ON MY SIDE, ALL THINGS ARE POSSIBLE

My Prayer

Father, I thank you for all you have done
You are my star, my moon, and even my sun
You have always been there for me since
day one
I thank you for my talent and all the joy who
have brought me
I thank you for my life, health, and my
family
You are always there for me I know I can
count of you
I know you are there to support me in
everything that I do
I look forward to talking with you again
This is my prayer oh Lord, Amen

Testimony

Second chances-I haven't always believed in
But Lord, you saved me and washed away
all of my sins
How blind I was for so many years
No longer sadness but joyful tears
I can see clearly now-I have reasons to live
I have so much more life to live and love to
give
You took me out of a life of despair
A life where only phonies were there
You've healed me and for that I'm a better
me
Thank you God, this is my testimony

My Best Friend

What an awesome being, you reign supreme
You and I, we make the perfect team
My best friend, my confidant-only you can I
depend
I know that no matter what you'll be with
me from beginning to end
You're bigger than life itself, how can I ever
thank you
My highlight of the day is getting on my
knees to praise you
I can't see you but I know you are always
with me
My protector, my father-you mean so much
to me
You've done so much-how can I ever repay
you
I can't wait for the day that I finally meet
you
What a time we're going to have
I'm pretty sure in the meantime we'll cross
paths
Just know, I love you and I thank you for all
the good and bad times I've had
You may not come when I want you to, but I
know you'll be there right on time
Don't you all wish you had a friend like
mine

All the Riches

Lord, I know I am blessed
Is something I say every day before I get
dressed
I have a roof over my head and food to eat
When I get cold at night, I am fortunate
enough to turn on the heat
I have loving parents who would do
anything for me
I have brothers and sisters who truly admire
me
Lord, you have given me a job that I
absolutely adore
You have given me a loving family that I
would die for
Lord, you've blessed me with everything
plus more
I don't have all the riches in the world
But still, I am a blessed girl
You see, I am rich because of all the
blessings that he bestows upon me
I know from the outside rich is not what you
see
My blessings outnumber any amount of cash
you'll ever have
Count your many blessings and then do the
math

The Lord Giveth and the Lord Taketh Away

Be careful who you worship, God is not a
job or even a car
He's not a boyfriend or a famous movie star
His name is almighty – not Chaps or Ralph
Lauren or any other materialistic thing
Have we forgotten it is God that grants us all
the joy that life may bring
It was God that got you that job that you
needed so desperately
It was God that got you that car, allowing
you to get from point a to b
It was God that was there when that special
someone left you
It was God that helped you buy those
expensive pair of shoes
No matter what, God is there through the
good and bad times
Remember when you were jobless, carless,
clothesless, and filled with loneliness -
sometimes we need to travel back in time
But as soon as we receive all that, we
quickly forget to fall to our knees
Even though God has given you all these
things
We still need to continue to worship Him,
study His holy word, and pray
You see God has a lot of jealous ways

He may giveth, but He may also taketh away

Dream Big, My Sister

How tall and firm you stand
With limbs as strong as a giant's hand
The winds may blow strong,
But my sister, keep the faith and hold on
Long gone-are our days as just a housewife
We're entrepreneurs-taking control of our
own life
My sisters are running things-and that's how
it should be
We all have powerful minds-if used
correctly
The world is filled with so much more
Take that opportunity when it knocks at
your door
You can fulfill your deepest fantasies
When you feel you can't make it, just fall
down on your knees
We've come a long way but the struggle still
exists
Black women vs. Black women, it all ends
in a fist
Instead of fighting each other
We should support one another
Use that energy to build a career
Being young, rich, and successful can be our
deepest fear
All of us are talented in a special way
With success, comes patience, dreams don't
get fulfilled in just a day

101

The message to my sisters-let's take over the world-and make our dreams come true
Dream big, my sister if it happened to me it can happen to you.

Get Up

We are all destined to do great things
Let's all dream big and live like queens and
kings
It doesn't matter what your situation may be
You can grow up to be anything you wish to
be
A doctor or a lawyer the possibilities are
endless
Let's try our best and strive for greatness
Don't let anyone stop your shine
Get up and do something, stay on your grind
Put God first in everything that you do
The rest is left up to you

Not What It Seems

He works and works-he works his life away
His primary goal in life is to be successful
one day
Family and friends-he just doesn't have the
time
Making it to the top is all that he has on his
mind
His loved ones constantly beg "let's spend
more time together"
His only concern is taking his career further
He just doesn't know how successful he
already is
He is blessed with a beautiful wife and three
kids
In which their patience is about to wear out
Because obviously he forgotten what love
was about

A couple months pass by and his career sails
On the flip side his family is fed up and bails
Selfishly he thought his career alone would
make him happy
Months go by and he realizes he misses his
family
He ponders how he can get back what he
just lost
Suddenly he realizes success comes at a cost
Swallowing his pride, he talks to his wife
trying to make things better

Assuring her that he wants his family in his
life from now until forever
She takes him back and he learns he has to
take time out for his loved ones
He begins by taking them out and having
some fun
A couple months past and he still has his job
but doesn't work as much as he used to
Now he knows, what is success if you have
no one to share it with you

To Everyone:
Chase your dreams, but in the process don't
chase your family and friends away.

Shake It Off

The world is filled with so much envy
On the job, at the church, even in our
families
What's sad- it happens mostly in our own
race
They'll stab you in the back then smile in
your face
What's on our agenda-all day everyday-hate
on another?
As a people, we've been through so much
we should all love each other
Instead we fight, hate, and back stab our
sisters and brothers
How can you look me in the face and still
betray me
The answer to that obviously-jealousy
That's why I only trust God and of course I
trust me
It's lonely sometimes but that's how it's got
to be
You can hate me but the moral is you won't
stop me
All you are doing for me is motivating me
See I'm going to be somebody regardless if
you support me
When I make it to the top-of course you'll
be on my thank you list
Because I'm glad I fought you with revenge
instead of my fist

You may hate me-but you'll never defeat me
You are just a devil in disguise
Wake up and realize
You can't stop me or my shine
Always I'll shake you off-I'm going for
mine

Break Me

Although your words may sometimes hurt
me
Jealousy and envy are all these brown eyes
see
You are rude to me and certainly don't have
any respect
But one day I'm going to make it big-and
that's a sure bet
Yeah your comments make me feel pretty
low
I sometimes cry, and at one point my
confidence was down to the floor
But I am stronger now-I had enough time to
grow
I've learned that you see me as a threat and
just want to break me
You have talked about me, disrespected me,
and treated me badly
Just know you can't break me, although you
have tried
One day during my lunch break I sat in my
car and cried
But that will never happen again-and this I
swear
One thing for certain, I am not going no
where
But to the top and that where I'm going to
stay

But until then just remember every dog has their day

Revenge

The sweet smell of it-don't you hate it
Even though you tried to stop me-I still
made it
Look at me, your girl has done good
With all the negativity around me-you
thinking how could?
I know, I know, you wished I had of
stumbled
But by the grace of God, I pressed on and I
remained humbled
And it isn't over; I'm headed straight to the
top
If memory serves me correctly you all said I
was going to flop
But don't think I'm doing this to get back at
you
For my drive, ambition, and grind I would
like to thank you
I would rather beat you with success than
with my fist
When it comes to thank you's you are on the
top of my list
I thank you for underestimating me-thinking
I wouldn't amount to much
Thank you for making me stronger, driven,
ambitious, and such
But look at me now, matter of fact take a
picture

Cause me now, is not the same person you
remember
They say success is the greatest victory
For all of you who never thought I would
amount to anything-look at me and you
know what you'll see
An educated, successful, strong, determined
young lady
So just know, your words and actions didn't
stop me
It only inspired me-so for that I thank you-
cause you made me a better me

Corporate America

We all want the American dream
Young, rich, and successful-but what does
all that mean
Selling our souls just to make it to the top
We would rather shake hands with the devil
than to flop
What good is the top if we didn't get their
fairly
How can you hold your head up high with
dignity?
Knowing all the people you stepped on to
get where you are
You may be successful now but surely you
won't make it far
You may lose yourself in the chase of
everything
Lie, cheat, backstab all for the American
dream
Sometimes success isn't quite what it seems
For the right price people will plot and
scheme
People will go to great lengths just to get
their shine
Willing to step over anybody especially their
own kind
Let's all be young, rich, and successful-but
let's get it the right way
Let's work hard, stay true to ourselves, and
especially pray

I want the American dream and I am dying
to get there
And when I do make it I can honestly say I
played it fair

Shadow

It's hard to escape it-even though it's several
years old
No matter how much you want to let go-it
has a strong hold
It's hard to overlook-when it's standing right
behind
Painful memories are hard to escape my
mind
Tell me how can I get rid of you
We've had a long ride-but as of right now
we're threw
You were never good for me
Matter fact you destroyed me
It's going to take years to fix this terrible
mess
You've caused me nothing but heartache
and sadness
Our departure is definitely what's best
I realized I don't need you anymore I've
found happiness
But know, you taught me to love myself-
inside and out
You taught me what true love was really all
about
You taught me that I didn't need to be
surrounded with negativity
You taught me to be real-to always be me
But I do thank you because without you I
wouldn't have found me

But now that I'm rid of you-I'm finally free

To everyone:
Don't let your past get in the way of your
future

Survivor

I've put up with a lot-too much as some
would argue
No one would believe all the ridiculous crap
I've been through
They try to bring me down but I always
bounce back time after time
They can hate all they want but no matter
what I'm going for mine
Jealousy and envy-I'm sorry but that's not a
characteristic of mine
Regardless of how low you make me feel-
I'm still here
And I don't care how big and bad you think
you are-it's only God that I fear
Your jealous ways does nothing but drive
me
And I won't stop at nothing until its success
that I see
They try to throw stones-demean my
character
I just fall on my knees-God always have an
answer
Through all the jealousy, ridicule, and
hatefulness-I'm a survivor
I walk with my head held high everyday
To my jealous ones-you can hate all you
want but guess what I'm here to stay.

Beat the Odds

Twenty six years ago two parents gave birth
to a beautiful baby boy
They named him Jeremiah, who brought
them so much joy
In the beginning they wanted the best for
their son
Shortly after, so called friends persuaded
them that they should go out and have their
own fun

They would soon get lost in the nightlife
And for several years live the highlife
Jeremiah was neglected and was always left
at home
He couldn't figure out why he was always
left alone
So many times he saw his parents stoned out
of their mind
There were so many pipes and needles he
would find
He missed his old parents and all the good
times

He ran away from home searching for love
elsewhere
His parents didn't notice that he wasn't there
He was embraced by a gang who promised
to take care of him

Even though they did bad things he still
loved each one of them
Because for the first time ever, he had
someone to love him

This one particular night they plan to rob a
store
The police catch them as they exit the door
Now Jeremiah is headed for jail
He has no one to visit, no one to post bail
As he sits behind bars he examines his life
As soon as he gets out he wants to make
things right
He wants to leave the gang and the street life

Months pass by and he is released
He plans to get his GED and pick up a trade
at least
Also he wants to visit his parents and make
up for lost time
And look past the memories that has
plagued his mind

As he prepares for his visit he contemplates
what to say
Please allow us to be a family again, dear
Lord to you I pray
As he opens the door he is surprised by what
he sees
He is greeted by a loving couple who was
not his family

He introduces himself and they proceed to
let him in
He soon finds out that they are actually kin

He asks about his parents and they replied
I'm so sorry to tell you this but they died
Shocked at the news he wish he could have
been there
He felt lost, like life was being unfair
The couple felt sorry for him and invited
him to live with them
They put him in school and supported him
He is focused now and everything is seen
clearly
Now he owns his own business and wants to
start his own family
At night he ends his day with a prayer,
"Thank you God for the obstacles I had to
overcome, for that made me a better me."

The Obstacle

You've never thought this could happen to
you
But here you are standing without a clue
You don't know what to do
Everything is beyond you

Wishing you had the knowledge to achieve
Instead you have the knowledge to
disbelieve
Trying to put your life behind
Knowing harmony you will find

Failure you need to defeat
And gain belief

Trapped in this gruesome obstacle course
With disbelief as your source
Trying to discover the right path
Thinking your life was cut in half

To Everyone:
Just pray and stay strong
Keep the faith and hold on
Life will not be easy
Joy comes in the morning, you'll see

Not a Friend of Mine

I see you on the street corners but you're
nothing to me
I roll right past in my all black e-class
proudly
What I need with your little weed, coke, or
ecstasy
I refuse to let anyone or anything get the
best of me
Just listen to me
I got big things I want to accomplish in my
lifetime
And last I checked, being a dope fiend was
not a goal of mine
I'm sorry but losing your family, friends,
yourself, and your soul just don't quite
impress me
Unlike many others I'm trying to be all that
God wants me to be
Life hasn't always been easy, but I played
the hand that was dealt
At 25, I've experienced love, joy, and the
greatest pain ever felt
Yeah I've had my problems but never once
would I touch you
I've seen firsthand the devastating damage
you can do
You've took so many lives both young and
old

It's ridiculous to think about all the innocent
lives you've stole
Life may sometimes throw obstacles your
way
But that don't mean you got to resort to
doing drugs every day
Talk your problems to God-He'll surely
understand
Otherwise the devil will have you eating out
the palm of his hands

Turning Point

These are supposed to be the best years of
my life-so they say
Well how come when I wake up every day
is just-another day
It's like something's missing-this isn't all
what I had hoped for
I thought at this point in my life I'll be worth
much more
This is not what I want to do-or who I want
to be
I want something better not only for me but
my family
It's time for something different-time to
make a change
And from this moment forward I will set
goals and accomplish them within a
reasonable time frame
It's time to stop talking but really be about it
Because when opportunity knocks this time
I certainly don't want to miss it
You read in the paper each and every day
about the passing of another
What I've learned from this is, don't take
any second for granted because you might
not
get another
Don't make any excuses, live out your
dreams

Reach for the sky, no matter how farfetched
it may seem
Only you can make a turning point from a
negative to a positive
Dream big and aim high because you are
only given one life to live.

My Promise

Mom, my best friend, my role model, oh
how I love you
I have you told you so many times but I'll
tell you once more-what would I do without
you
You have helped me in so many ways how
can I ever repay you
If I ever lost you I don't know what I'll do
I've always admired how you take charge of
things
You always remain calm no matter how
tough situations may seem
I thank you for always being there and
loving me
When I make it big I'll fulfill all your
dreams-you'll see

Dad, we have always been close, we are a
perfect pair
You sometimes were strict but that shows
you care
In the past we didn't quite see eye to eye
But how young, foolish, and naive was I
If I ever have a son I hope he's just like you
I may not always tell you but Daddy I love
you
Dad, I will always be your little girl, no
matter how old I may be

You have always wanted the very best for
me
When I make it big I'll fulfill all your
dreams-you'll see

Made in the USA
Columbia, SC
12 August 2020

16178150R00070